THE DOCTRINE OF MAN

This series examines the doctrine of man. It starts with his creation and ends with his climax, the perfect man, the Lord Jesus Christ.

The Record of Creation

The biblical account of the creation of man is found in the opening chapters of Genesis. Although the account was written many years after the events to which it relates and Moses[1] (obviously) was not an eyewitness of either the creation of the world or the formation of Adam, there is no need to doubt the accuracy of the account.

There are a number of reasons for this. First, the Lord Jesus affirmed the accuracy of Moses' account (Matthew 19:4; Mark 13:19). Since Christians hold that the Lord Jesus was the Son of God which of necessity means He was infallible, His authority

[1]Although the book itself does not say that it was written by Moses, his authorship is mentioned in the N.T. e.g. Jn. 1:17, as is his authorship of the other books of the Pentateuch. Ex. 17:14; 24:4; Num. 33:2; Deut. 31:9, 22 and 24 show that he was a writer. Although it is probably true that many of the Patriarchs lived in days before reading and writing were common skills, Moses was reared in Pharaoh's palace where he would have been taught to read and write.

stands behind the account of creation in Genesis. Second, the idea of creation is consistent with belief in an all-powerful God. The account of creation ex *nihilo* is only doubtful if the existence of God is doubtful. But if it is recognised that the creation of man was no more difficult and probably somewhat simpler than the creation of the cosmos, then the record of Genesis is not inherently improbable. A person who believes in God should not find the idea that God created man difficult. Third, the account of creation purports to be factual. There is no hint that its author intended it to be understood as allegory. It contains for example genealogies[2] (nine in total) which link together the characters of the Book. Although biblical genealogies occasionally "jump" a generation they belong to a historical rather than fictional genre of literature. Moreover the accounts of the lives of people such as Abraham, Isaac, Jacob and Joseph are far removed from the extraordinary and fantastical accounts of creation found in pagan mythology.

Moses probably wrote Genesis during the Wilderness years after the Law had been given and God's moral standards had been laid down. His account of the misbehaviour of his forefathers would have been written with a clear understanding of God's disapproval of adultery, murder etc. Nevertheless these failures are recorded unflinchingly. Moses was obviously not trying to "whitewash" his nation's history. In these circumstances it is reasonable to think that whoever wrote the book was seeking to tell the truth in both his account of creation as well as his account of the development of the Nation of Israel. Then, of course, there is the bulwark of divine inspiration. Scripture claims the status of infallibility (Jn. 10:34; 2 Tim. 3:16). The account of man's creation is found in a book inspired by God.

The account of the creation of man is part of a more general account of creation. The record does not state how God created all things save to indicate that He had the power and wisdom to accomplish it. While no doubt the scientific details could have been supplied, the account was written by Moses to inform his own Nation of their origins. It was not written to explain creation from a scientific perspective. He did not and could not within the limits of Hebrew vocabulary or understanding

---

[2]Genesis 5:1–32 (Adam to Noah) 10:1–32 (The sons of Noah and their descendants), 11:10–26 (Noah's son Shem to Abram), 11:27–32 (The descendants of Terah), 22:20–24 (The descendants of Nahor), 25:1–4 (The descendants of Abraham by Keturah), 25:12–18 (The descendants of Ishmael), 35:23–29 (The descendants of Jacob), 36:1–43 (The descendants of Esau).

have provided a scientific explanation of the sort that today's physicists or biologists would find acceptable. The creation account is not meant to be a scientific account.

While the universe and world were created from nothing, man was created from material God had already created. God used the "dust" to make Adam. On death he still returns to dust. This may have been because God wished to demonstrate that he belonged to the world into which he was placed. By what process the dust was transformed into flesh, sinew and muscle we are not told. The word "Adam" is a Hebrew word for "man". Since all of mankind was potentially in Adam the word sometimes means mankind i.e. male and female (Gen. 1:27). It is first used as a proper name in Genesis 2 verse 19. Likewise, woman was made from existing material. But she was created from living material; the bone and tissue of Adam's rib. Genesis does not state why God did not use dust when He made Eve but in context the point was to emphasise that she was derived from him and was designed to help him (Gen. 2:18). Writers in the New Testament base their teaching about the relationship between the sexes on the fact that man was the first to be created (1 Cor. 11:9; 1 Tim. 2:13). Matthew Henry's observation in this connection is worth quoting. "The woman was made of a rib out of the side of Adam; not made out of his head to rule over him, nor out of his feet to be trampled upon by him, but out of his side to be equal with him, under his arm to be protected, and near his heart to be beloved."[3] Eve means "living" hence "mother of all living" (Gen. 3:20).

Although the evolution of mankind is now regarded by many as a fact as opposed to a theoretical account of how creation might have happened, Christians start from a different premise. If there is a God He is by definition infinitely powerful and wise. God has no need to superintend an elongated evolutionary process in order to bring about His purposes. While there is no doubt that species adapt to their environment and change in a variety of ways over time this does not mean that the account of creation should be discarded.

---

[3]Matthew Henry's Commentary on the Whole Bible (Hendrickson) p. 10.

The Reason for Creation

This must first be considered from God's point of view. Since God knew before creation that man would rebel against Him and that He would have to judge man for that rebellion, we might wonder why He created man in the first place. But the knowledge that His creatures would rebel and would ultimately be judged was evidently not a reason for remaining in "splendid isolation" or to fashion a creature without the capacity to obey or disobey. We cannot judge the wisdom of that choice. But as believers we must be glad that He made it.

Although it is a fundamental issue, scripture has little to say about God's reason for creating man. The clearest statement comes from the lips of the elders in Revelation when they say, "thou hast created all things, and for thy pleasure they are and were created' (Rev. 4:11; cf. Col 1:16). Elsewhere, Isaiah quotes the words of God, "I have created him for my glory, I have formed him; yea, I have made him" (Is 43:7). Although in the immediate context Isaiah is speaking of the redeemed nation, the words are obviously meant to have a wider meaning. This is consistent with the purpose of creation generally (Ps. 8:3, 6, 9; 19:1-3). We may deduce from this that the Christian exists to bring glory to God (Eph. 1:12). Thus although God did not need to create man and does not depend on us, He can receive back from us something that pleases Him. This means that there is a reason for living and a purpose to life. Of course, when we recollect that apart from the death of the Saviour we would not be able to glorify God, the wonder is that He ever created us at all.

Thus our purpose must be to fulfil the reason why God created us: to glorify Him. But we also find that in doing so we find personal fulfilment and satisfaction. The Bible describes the life of the unsaved as futile (1 Peter 1:18). The life of the Christian is by contrast a life of fulfilment and satisfaction – discontented Christians are men and women who have failed to realise God's purpose for their life.

 ## KEY SCRIPTURES

26 And God said, Let us make man in our image, after our likeness: and let them have dominion over the fish of the sea, and over the fowl of the air, and over the cattle, and over all the earth, and over every creeping thing that creepeth upon the earth. 27 So God created man in his *own* image, in the image of God created he him; male and female created he them. 28 And God blessed them, and God said unto them, Be fruitful, and multiply, and replenish the earth, and subdue it: and have dominion over the fish of the sea, and over the fowl of the air, and over every living thing that moveth upon the earth. 29 And God said, Behold, I have given you every herb bearing seed, which *is* upon the face of all the earth, and every tree, in the which *is* the fruit of a tree yielding seed; to you it shall be for meat. 30 And to every beast of the earth, and to every fowl of the air, and to everything that creepeth upon the earth, wherein *there is* life, *I have given* every green herb for meat: and it was so.

Gen 1:26-30

7 And the LORD God formed man *of* the dust of the ground, and breathed into his nostrils the breath of life; and man became a living soul.

Gen 2:7

1 This *is* the book of the generations of Adam. In the day that God created man, in the likeness of God made he him; 2 Male and female created he them; and blessed them, and called their name Adam, in the day when they were created. 3 And Adam lived an hundred and thirty years, and begat *a son* in his own likeness, after his image; and called his name Seth:

Gen 5:1–3

📖 KEY SCRIPTURES

6 I will say to the north, Give up; and to the south, Keep not back: bring my sons from far, and my daughters from the ends of the earth; 7 *Even every one that is called by my name: for I have created him for my glory. I have formed him; yea, I have made him.*

Isaiah 43:6–7

4 ...he hath chosen us in him before the foundation of the world, that we should be holy and without blame before him in love: 5 Having predestinated us unto the adoption of children by Jesus Christ to himself, according to the good pleasure of his will,

Eph 1:4–5

11 In whom also we have obtained an inheritance, being predestinated according to the purpose of him who worketh all things after the counsel of his own will: 12 That we should be to the praise of his glory, who first trusted in Christ.

Eph 1:11–12

16 For by him were all things created, that are in heaven, and that are in earth, visible and invisible, whether *they be* thrones, or dominions, or principalities, or powers: all things were created by him, and for him:

Col 1:16

11 Thou art worthy, O Lord, to receive glory and honour and power: for thou hast created all things, and for thy pleasure they are and were created.

Rev 4:11

 KEY QUOTES

One's view of the origin of man will affect his entire understanding of and attitude toward man. If, for instance, man is the product of evolution, then the extent of the effects of sin and the need of a Saviour are played down, if not eliminated. If, on the other hand, man was created by God, then this concept carries with it the companion idea of the responsibility of man. If God created man, then there is someone outside of man to whom he becomes responsible. He is not in and of himself the master of his own fate or completely at the mercy of fate; he is neither the final authority nor the only one to whom he must ultimately answer. A doctrine of creation implies creatures who are responsible to that Creator. The evolutionary origin of man relieves man of responsibility to a personal Creator outside of himself.[4]

Charles Ryrie

Understanding the doctrine of the creation of man has very practical results. When we realise that God creates us to glorify Him, and when we start to act in ways that fulfil that purpose, then we begin to experience an intensity of joy in the Lord that we have never known before. When we add to that the realisation that God Himself is rejoicing in our fellowship with Him, our joy becomes "inexpressible and filled with heavenly glory" (1 Peter 1:8 author's paraphrase).[5]

Wayne Grudem

What is the chief and highest end of man? Man's chief and highest end is to glorify God, and fully to enjoy Him for ever.

Westminster Larger Catechism.

---

[4]Charles Caldwell Ryrie, *A Survey of Bible Doctrine* (Moody Press).
[5]Bible Doctrine (IVP) p 189.

KEY QUESTIONS

1. How did Moses know how the world was created?

2. In the story of creation we learn about the "tree of life", "the tree of the knowledge of good and evil" and a garden named "Eden". Were they actual trees and was Eden a real place? How would you prove your answer?

3. Why did God create man?

4. What lessons can be learnt from the differing ways in which man and woman are created?

MAN'S NATURE AND HIS FALL

Man's Nature

Man was made in the "image of God" (Gen. 1:26; 5:1). What does "image" mean? It cannot mean a physical resemblance for God is a spirit. The meaning of the phrase can be deduced from the fact that none of the other creatures mentioned in Genesis are said to have been made in God's image. What made man different from them? The answer is that man resembled God because he was a spiritual being with a consciousness of good and evil. He was capable of reason and had a will.

Being made in God's image separates man from creation. This is reflected in a variety of ways. The Bible does not condemn the killing of animals but killing another human is condemned because it involves destroying someone who has some of God's features (Gen. 9:6). The unique status of man means that he is entitled to respect. Thus a fetus in the womb even though it has not developed sufficiently to be conscious of God or to know the difference between good and evil is still made in God's image and hence worthy of protection. It is enough that the fetus or baby belongs to mankind. Likewise, at the end of life a person with Alzheimer's Disease is worthy of respect for the same reason. We cannot treat humans as we would treat the brute creation. That is not to say that creation is not worthy of respect. It is an inheritance from the Lord. Creation is an expression of

God's greatness and goodness. There is no merit in polluting, exploiting or hunting it to the point of extinction.

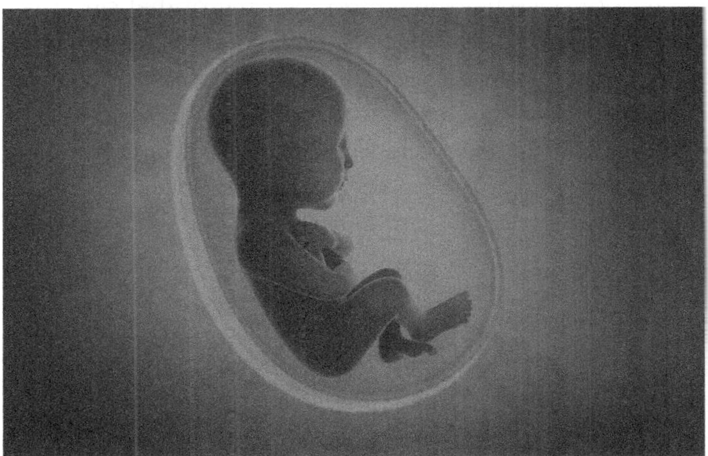

The Lord Jesus gave perfect expression to God's image in humanity (Heb. 1:3). Christians should display the image of God in their life (2 Cor 3:18) and one day will be perfectly conformed to that image (Rom 8:29).

The Fall

When Adam and Eve sinned, this led to a series of catastrophic spiritual and physical consequences for them and also for the world they inhabited. We call the moment when man disobeyed God "the Fall" – although it is not an expression used in scripture, it is useful shorthand for the consequences of their disobedience to God. The principal consequence is that they developed a sinful nature. What had been a latent possibility became an active instinct. Before they sinned Adam and Eve were innocent. Young children go through a similar phase. But Adam and Eve succumbed to sin in a perfect environment. Children see and hear the effects of sin from their birth. They are tempted to sin from early days. But in addition the Bible teaches that unlike our first parents they inherit a fallen nature (Ps. 51:5). The Bible does not explain whether the fallen nature is transmitted in the same way DNA is passed on from parent to child or whether it is passed on from parent to child in some other way. But prior to the Fall they had lived in innocence (that is, they could sin but did not sin). After the Fall they became fallen creatures (that is, they could not, not sin). The

Roman epistle teaches not only that all sin but that we all inherit Adam's guilt. There is corporate responsibility in humanity for Adam's sin (Rom. 5:12, 19). All that have been born since have inherited the guilt of that sin. His corruption is absolute and complete and he cannot do anything that would earn him favour in God's sight. This is sometimes called the doctrine of the total depravity of man. This does not mean that everyone is as thoroughly depraved in his actions as he could possibly be, nor that everyone will indulge in every form of sin, nor that a person cannot appreciate and even do acts of goodness; but it does mean that the corruption of sin extends to all men and to all parts of all men.

KEY SCRIPTURES

[26] And God said, Let us make man in our image, after our likeness.... [27] So God created man in his *own* image, in the image of God created he him; male and female created he them...

Gen 1:26-27

[6] Whoso sheddeth man's blood, by man shall his blood be shed: for in the image of God made he man.

Gen 9:6

[29] For whom he did foreknow, he also did predestinate *to be* conformed to the image of his Son, that he might be the firstborn among many brethren. [30] Moreover whom he did predestinate, them he also called: and whom he called, them he also justified: and whom he justified, them he also glorified.

Rom 8:29-30

[6] For if the woman be not covered, let her also be shorn: but if it be a shame for a woman to be shorn or shaven, let her be covered. [7] For a man indeed ought not to cover *his* head, forasmuch as he is the image and glory of God: but the woman is the glory of the man.

1 Cor 11:6-7

18 But we all, with open face beholding as in a glass the glory of the Lord, are changed into the same image from glory to glory, *even* as by the Spirit of the Lord.

2 Cor 3:18

8 But now ye also put off all these; anger, wrath, malice, blasphemy, filthy communication out of your mouth. 9 Lie not one to another, seeing that ye have put off the old man with his deeds; 10 And have put on the new *man*, which is renewed in knowledge after the image of him that created him: 11 Where there is neither Greek nor Jew, circumcision nor uncircumcision, Barbarian, Scythian, bond *nor* free: but Christ *is* all, and in all.

Col 3:8-11

8 But the tongue can no man tame; *it is* an unruly evil, full of deadly poison. 9 Therewith bless we God, even the Father; and therewith curse we men, which are made after the similitude of God.

James 3:8-9

"Surely I was sinful at birth, sinful from the time my mother conceived me"

Psalm 51:5 [NIV]

10 As it is written, There is none righteous, no, not one: 11 There is none that understandeth, there is none that seeketh after God. 12 They are all gone out of the way, they are together become unprofitable; there is none that doeth good, no, not one.

Rom 3:10–12

...by one man sin entered into the world, and death by sin; and so death passed upon all men, for that all have sinned:

Rom 5:12

KEY SCRIPTURES

22 For as in Adam all die, even so in Christ shall all be made alive.

1 Cor 15:22

1 And you *hath he quickened*, who were dead in trespasses and sins; 2 Wherein in time past ye walked according to the course of this world, according to the prince of the power of the air, the spirit that now worketh in the children of disobedience: 3 Among whom also we all had our conversation in times past in the lusts of our flesh, fulfilling the desires of the flesh and of the mind; and were by nature the children of wrath, even as others.

Eph 2:1-3

KEY QUOTES

The image of God extends to everything in which the nature of man surpasses that of all other species of animals. Accordingly, by this term is denoted the integrity with which Adam was endued when his intellect was clear, his affections subordinated to reason, all his senses duly regulated, and when he truly ascribed all his excellence to the admirable gifts of his Maker.… It cannot be doubted that when Adam lost his first estate he became alienated from God. Wherefore, although we grant that the image of God was not utterly effaced and destroyed in him, it was, however, so corrupted, that anything which remains is fearful deformity; and, therefore, our deliverance begins with that renovation which we obtain from Christ, who is, therefore, called the second Adam, because He restores us to true and substantial integrity. 6

Calvin

6Calvin, J., *Institutes of the Christian Religion.*

It will be seen that the scriptural doctrine of the Fall altogether contradicts the popular modern view of man as a being who, by a slow evolutionary development, has succeeded in rising from the primeval fear and groping ignorance of a humble origin to proud heights of religious sensitivity and insight. The Bible does not portray man as risen, but as fallen and in the most desperate of situations. It is only against this background that God's saving action in Christ takes on its proper significance. Through the grateful appropriation by faith of Christ's atoning work, what was forfeited by the Fall is restored to man: his true and intended dignity is recovered, the purpose of life recaptured, the image of God restored, and the way into the paradise of intimate communion with God reopened.[7]

New Bible Dictionary

What do we mean by total depravity? First, we do not mean…that all men and women are as thoroughly bad and depraved as they can possibly be… Second, it does not even mean that men and women in their fallen state have no innate knowledge of God, because they have…. Third, it does not mean that men and women do not have a conscience; therefore, it does not mean that they have no knowledge of good and evil. People in a state of total depravity do have a conscience, and they recognise the difference between good and evil…. Total depravity does not mean that men and women are incapable of recognising or admiring virtues, or that they are incapable of disinterested feelings and actions.

It means that man in his fallen condition has an inherently corrupt nature, and the corruption extends through every part of his being, to every faculty of his soul and body. It also means that there is no (observe the adjective) *spiritual* good in him. Yes, there is plenty of natural good, there

---

[7]*New Bible Dictionary*, p.360.

is natural morality, he can recognise virtue and so on. But there is no spiritual good whatsoever. .... To put it another way, all that person's powers are misused and perverted. [8]

Martyn Lloyd-Jones

---

[8]Lloyd-Jones, D. M. *God the Father, God the Son* p. 201-202.

KEY QUESTIONS

1. Does a human being differ from an animal and if so in what ways?

2. What changed after Adam and Eve disobeyed God?

3. What is meant by the expression "the Fall"?

4. Can a person choose not to sin?

MAN'S CONSTITUTION

The Bible teaches that man is composed of body, soul and spirit.

> And the very God of peace sanctify you wholly; and *I pray God* your whole spirit and soul and body be preserved blameless unto the coming of our Lord Jesus Christ. **1 Thess. 5:23**

Non-Christian thought argues that the only form of life that matters is the life of the body and that man ceases to exist on death. If this is so then man is the same as the plant in the garden or the tree of the field. All that gives them life is their physical existence. The Bible distinguishes between plant life and living creatures. Every living creature has a "soul" (Gen. 1:20, 21, 30; 2:7, 19; 9:4). The distinction between plant life and animal life is that "living creatures" are capable of thought, emotions and will. In the Old Testament when the word "soul" (*nepes*) is used in connection with man it also carries with it the idea of God-consciousness. In the New Testament another word is added – "spirit". The word "spirit" and "soul" are at times used interchangeably. For example, the Lord Jesus said, "Now is my soul troubled" (Jn 12:27) but in the next chapter John says that He was "troubled in spirit" (Jn 13:21). Mary says, "My <u>soul</u> doth magnify the Lord and my <u>spirit</u> hath rejoiced in God my Saviour" (Lk 1:46-47). The spirit relates to God (Ps. 103:1; Luke 1:46;) and lives forever (Rev. 6:9). It endures after physical death (Gen 35:18; Ps 31:5; Lk 23:43, 46; Acts 7:59;

Phil 1:23-24; 2 Cor 5:8 etc). Although animals have "souls" in the broad sense they do not have a spirit since the spirit enables an appreciation of divine things.

The language of 1 Thessalonians 5 verse 23 suggests that when used precisely, "soul" and "spirit" are distinguishable. Hebrews 4 verse 12 indicates that though the soul and spirit are closely intertwined, they may be divided.

The soul is given by God at conception (Heb. 12:9; Zech. 12:1; Isa. 42:5; cf. Ps. 139:13). This truth combined with God's supervision of the development of the fetus in the womb is a powerful reason for protecting the unborn child.

Man's constitution differs from angels. Angels are not born. They are created. They were all created at the same moment and are without number (Dan. 7:10; Heb 12:22). They do not die (Matt. 22:30). Although they can appear in human form (Matt 28:5; Heb. 13:2), they do not have physical bodies like ours (Heb. 1:14). They are spirit beings.

The diagram below depicts the differences between the role of body, soul and spirit. In reality they interact with and overlap one another.

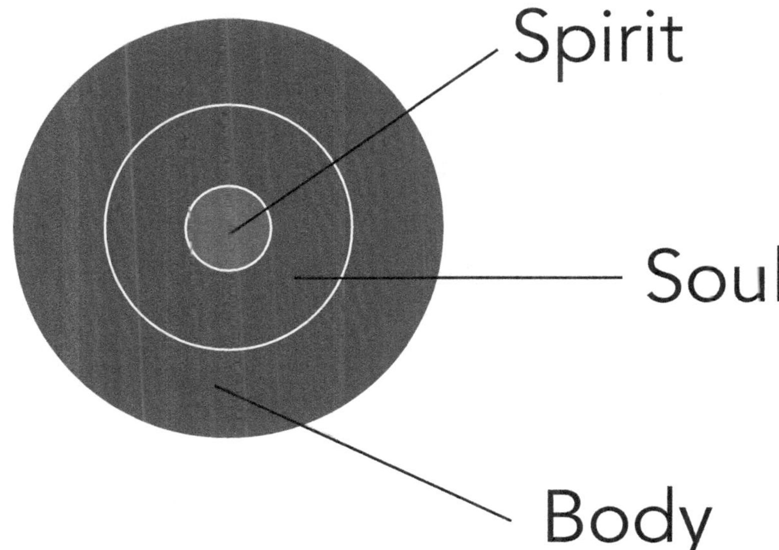

Body	**Soul**	**Spirit**
1. The five senses	1. Reason	1. Revelation from God
2. The motor skills (movement, manipulation of objects etc)	2. Emotion	2. Prayer to God
	3. Will	3. Communion with God
	4. Memory	4. Fellowship with saints
	5. Imagination	5. Spiritual inner senses/ knowledge/conscience
	6. Curiosity	6. Spiritual fruit
	7. Perception	7. Spiritual gifts
	8. Desires	8. Spiritual warfare

 ## KEY SCRIPTURES

7 And the LORD God formed man *of* the dust of the ground, and breathed into his nostrils the breath of life; and man became a living soul.

Gen 2:7

30 And to every animal of the earth, and to every fowl of the heavens, and to everything that creepeth on the earth, in which is a living soul, every green herb for food. And it was so.

Gen 1:30 (J.N.D.)

23 And the very God of peace sanctify you wholly; and *I pray God* your whole spirit and soul and body be preserved blameless unto the coming of our Lord Jesus Christ.

1 Thess 5:23

12 For the word of God *is* quick, and powerful, and sharper than any twoedged sword, piercing even to the dividing asunder of soul and spirit, and of the joints and marrow, and *is* a discerner of the thoughts and intents of the heart.

Heb 4:12

7 And of the angels he saith, Who maketh his angels spirits,

Heb 1:7

KEY QUOTES

Soul, spirit, heart, mind, will and conscience are all facets of man's immaterial nature, and it is often difficult to make hard and fast distinctions between them. It seems to be an oversimplification to say that man is body, soul and spirit, for soul and spirit do not fully categorize the immaterial part of man, and they are not always distinct. For instance, we are told to love God with the soul (Mt 22:37), and the flesh wars against the soul (1 Pet. 2:11). The spirit can magnify the Lord (Lk 1:46-47), and yet it can partake of corruption (2 Cor 7:1). In some instances it appears that the spirit is related to higher aspects of man's nature (and all men, including the unsaved, have a spirit, 1 Cor 2:11).[9]

Charles Ryrie

When a plant dies its material organization is dissolved and the... life which it contained disappears. When (an animal) dies its body returns to dust, and the (soul)... by which it was animated, passes away. When a man dies his body returns to the earth, his (soul) ceases to exist, his (spirit), alone remains until reunited with the body at the resurrection. To the (spirit), which is peculiar to man, belong reason, will, and conscience. To the (soul) which we have in common with (animals), belong understanding, feeling, and sensibility, or, the power of sense-perceptions. To the (soul) belongs what is purely material.[10]

Charles Hodge

[9] *A Survey of Bible Doctrine*
[10] Hodge, C. *Vol. 2: Systematic Theology* p. 47.

??? KEY QUESTIONS

1. What happens to man's body, soul and spirit on death?

2. Is a human being just the sum of his or her physical properties? If not how would you prove your answer?

3. If the body returns to dust at death, does that mean that God has no further use for the body?

4. What are the distinctions between the soul and spirit (if any)?

MAN'S COMPLEMENT

The title of this series of studies is *The Doctrine of Man*. "Man" in this connection means mankind in general whether male or female. In this chapter we will examine what the Bible has to say about the relationship between males and females, the two sexes which make up mankind.

The Bible teaches that God made males and females. The first creation account (Gen. 1:1-2:3) gives a brief overview of God's creative work. The second creation account (Gen. 2:4-25) reprises the first creation account with particular emphasis on the creation of man and woman. If all we had was the first account we might think that males and females were made simultaneously (Gen. 1:27). The second creation account however makes it clear that God created Adam before He created Eve. Thus God followed a different course with Adam and Eve from the course followed with other species. Scripture says that God created a woman to be a "help" to him (Gen. 2:18). His period alone may have been to impress on him how much a help she was. Since God "helps" man in scripture (e.g. 1 Sam. 7:12; Ps. 54:4; Heb. 13:6; cf. Rom. 16:3), it should not be thought that in filling this role there is any thought of inferiority. She was also made to be "meet" or suitable for him. She was biologically designed (as he had already been designed) to enable procreation. Had she never been given to Adam he would have had no descendants. Together they could procreate and build a relationship that was mutually beneficial physically, spiritually and emotionally.

The theory of evolution struggles to come up with an explanation of how two sexes evolved and evolved in a such way as to interact beneficially with one another. The Bible says that man was created by God from the dust of the earth and that woman was created from organic material derived from Adam, specifically his "rib". The method of formation has strong allegorical tones. That God chose to use a rib should not cause us to doubt the method chosen but rather it should cause us to discern the meaning of the method chosen. The method symbolises the derivative nature of the relationship between the male and female and also in taking her from the space beside his heart, the emotional relationship between them. As we have noticed in the first study in this series, the Lord Jesus and the apostle Paul spoke of Adam as having been created. Those who are committed to the infallibility of scripture or who consider that the Lord Jesus could not be mistaken about issues of this nature cannot therefore accept the evolutionary account of the origin of males and females.

Scripture later emphasises that the fact that God made woman for man exposes God's intentions in connection with the relationship between the sexes (see 1 Cor 11:9). In making man first and then providing woman to be a support to him a pattern was laid down that extends to govern the relationship between the sexes generally and in particular their roles in the institution of marriage and in the church. Broadly speaking scripture assigns the role of leadership to men in the confines of marriage and the Church. By contrast, women are assigned the role of nurturers in those spheres. Women bear children and are designed to be the primary givers of care to children. In the Church their gifts are ones which equip them to offer care and support. Scripture nowhere supports the idea that this is an inferior role. It is modelled on the relationship between the Father and the Son. Thus although the Son was equal in nature to the Father, He voluntarily assumed the role.

The relationship between the sexes in the church is also influenced by events post-creation. The fact that the woman was the first to be tempted and did not resist the temptation as she should have done is treated by Paul as a factor that determined the pattern of the relationship between the sexes in the church (1 Tim. 2:14). Whether other factors are involved is a matter for debate. Some had thought that since men are more truth orientated and women more relationship orientated, the responsibility for teaching and preserving truth is committed to man.

Although Genesis and parallel New Testament passages do emphasise the fact that man was created first and then woman created to provide someone who would support him, it does not follow that women are any less spiritual or valuable to God (Gal. 3:28). One of the features of the Church age is that it broke with the ethnic, religious and social distinctions that are characteristic of the Old Testament. Paul in particular taught the value of equality for those in Christ. Thus the slave enjoys equal place with the Master. The Jew with the Greek. The educated with the cultured and the male with the female (Col. 3:11). Another witness to the new appreciation of women is the respect they receive in the Gospels. Mary is a more prominent figure than Joseph in the life of the Lord Jesus and is portrayed as having a greater insight into the true nature of the Lord Jesus than that possessed by his family or the religious leaders of the day. Women on the whole showed a higher appreciation of Him than men. Women were first to His tomb after the resurrection (Matt. 28:1) and the men came later.

It is nevertheless the case that males and females are given different roles in the New Testament. Leadership in the Church was given to male apostles (Matt. 10:2). Leadership in the local church was given to male overseers (1 Tim. 3:2-11). Men are told to take the lead in the church in prayer (1 Tim. 2:8). The apostle Paul specifically prohibits women from teaching or more generally taking authority over men (1 Tim. 2:12) and says that they should be silent (1 Cor. 14:34) thus excluding audible participation on the gatherings. Scripture describes man as the head of the woman in Paul's discussion of their roles in the church (1 Cor. 11:3). In the context of marriage the husband is also described as the head (Eph. 5:23). Headship is not the same as lordship. Lordship emphasises authority and control whereas headship emphasises voluntary submission and reciprocal affection. Scripture nowhere teaches that man should dominate women by physical force or emotional dominance. The horrors of domestic violence are abhorrent to God's model of the proper relationship between husband and wife (Eph. 5:25).

Feminism is a movement that seeks to remove male dominance in society and its institutions and promote equality between the sexes. Feminism began to gain influence in the 19th Century in Western Europe and the USA. Much of its work is consistent with the broad Christian belief in the equality of all people in the eyes of

God (Rom. 2:11; Eph. 6:9). Thus the right to own property, to vote and the right to be treated equally in the workplace is consistent with Christian values. More difficult however is the move to equalise the roles of men and women in the Church.

Women's rights groups have campaigned for access to contraception and abortion, both of which raise problematic issues. Another consequence of the drive for equality has been a blurring of society's traditional commitment to distinctive dress codes for male and female.   Feminist theologians have objected to God being described as a male called "the Father" and are unhappy that Jesus is described as "the Son". While it is true that God is a spirit and cannot be assigned a gender, the scriptures do describe all three persons of the trinity in the masculine gender. The Holy Spirit is described in terms of the male gender (even though Spirit is neuter word). To alter the language God has chosen to describe Himself is to meddle with divine choices and alter scripture. "Gender neutral" translations of the Bible seek to remove signs of male domination from scripture. Some of the changes are probably unimportant e.g. the word *anthropos* "man" is translated "mankind" or "humankind" so as to make it obvious that both male and female are in view. But some of the changes blur the difference between the sexes and their respective roles.

KEY SCRIPTURES

[18] And the LORD God said, *It is* not good that the man should be alone; I will make him an help meet for him. [19] And out of the ground the LORD God formed every beast of the field, and every fowl of the air; and brought *them* unto Adam to see what he would call them: and whatsoever Adam called every living creature, that *was* the name thereof. [20] And Adam gave names to all cattle, and to the fowl of the air, and to every beast of the field; but for Adam there was not found an help meet for him. [21] And the LORD God caused a deep sleep to fall upon Adam, and he slept: and he took one of his ribs, and closed up the flesh instead thereof; [22] And the rib, which the LORD God had taken from man, made he a woman, and brought her unto the man. [23] And Adam said, This *is* now bone of my bones, and flesh of my flesh: she shall be called Woman, because she was taken out of Man. [24] Therefore shall a man leave his father and his mother, and shall cleave unto his wife: and they shall be one flesh.

Gen 2:18–24

[3] But I would have you know, that the head of every man is Christ; and the head of the woman *is* the man; and the head of Christ *is* God.

1 Cor 11:3

[8] …the first man didn't come from woman, but the first woman came from man. [9] And man was not made for woman, but woman was made for man. [10] For this reason, and because the angels are watching, a woman should wear a covering on her head to show she is under authority. [11] But among the Lord's people, women are not independent of men, and men are not independent of women. [12] For although the first woman came from man, every other man was born from a woman, and everything comes from God.

1 Cor 11:8–12 (NLT)

KEY SCRIPTURES

¹¹ Let the woman learn in silence with all subjection. ¹² But I suffer not a woman to teach, nor to usurp authority over the man, but to be in silence. ¹³ For Adam was first formed, then Eve. ¹⁴ And Adam was not deceived, but the woman being deceived was in the transgression. ¹⁵ Notwithstanding she shall be saved in childbearing, if they continue in faith and charity and holiness with sobriety.

1 Tim 2:11–15

If anyone sets his heart on being an overseer, he desires a noble task. ² Now the overseer must be above reproach, the husband of but one wife, temperate, self-controlled, respectable, hospitable, able to teach, ³ not given to drunkenness, not violent but gentle, not quarrelsome, not a lover of money. ⁴ He must manage his own family well and see that his children obey him with proper respect. ⁵ (If anyone does not know how to manage his own family, how can he take care of God's church?) ⁶ He must not be a recent convert, or he may become conceited and fall under the same judgment as the devil. ⁷ He must also have a good reputation with outsiders, so that he will not fall into disgrace and into the devil's trap. ⁸ Deacons, likewise, are to be men worthy of respect, sincere, not indulging in much wine, and not pursuing dishonest gain. ⁹ They must keep hold of the deep truths of the faith with a clear conscience. ¹⁰ They must first be tested; and then if there is nothing against them, let them serve as deacons. ¹¹ In the same way, their wives are to be women worthy of respect, not malicious talkers but temperate and trustworthy in everything. ¹² A deacon must be the husband of but one wife and must manage his children and his household well. ¹³ Those who have served well gain an excellent standing and great assurance in their faith in Christ Jesus.

1 Tim 3:1–13 (N.I.V.)

KEY SCRIPTURES

22 Wives, submit yourselves unto your own husbands, as unto the Lord. 23 For the husband is the head of the wife, even as Christ is the head of the church: and he is the saviour of the body. 24 Therefore as the church is subject unto Christ, so *let* the wives *be* to their own husbands in every thing. 25 Husbands, love your wives, even as Christ also loved the church, and gave himself for it....; 28 So ought men to love their wives as their own bodies. He that loveth his wife loveth himself.... 31 For this cause shall a man leave his father and mother, and shall be joined unto his wife, and they two shall be one flesh.

Eph 5:22–31

24 And a certain Jew named Apollos, born at Alexandria, an eloquent man, *and* mighty in the scriptures, came to Ephesus. 25 This man was instructed in the way of the Lord; and being fervent in the spirit, he spake and taught diligently the things of the Lord, knowing only the baptism of John. 26 And he began to speak boldly in the synagogue: whom when Aquila and Priscilla had heard, they took him unto *them*, and expounded unto him the way of God more perfectly.

Acts 18:24–26

3 ... aged women likewise, that *they be* in behaviour as becometh holiness, not false accusers, not given to much wine, teachers of good things; 4 That they may teach the young women to be sober, to love their husbands, to love their children, 5 *To be* discreet, chaste, keepers at home, good, obedient to their own husbands, that the word of God be not blasphemed.

Titus 2:3–5

27 For as many of you as have been baptized into Christ have put on Christ. 28 There is neither Jew nor Greek, there is neither bond nor free, there is neither male nor female: for ye are all one in Christ Jesus.

Gal 3:27–28

KEY QUOTES

In the religious world, feminists sought to update the language of the Bible and God to accommodate their new feminist consciousness. Although the Bible "contained" God's words for humanity, feminists believed that it contained, to a greater extent, the words of men for the self-perpetuation of patriarchy .... Feminists therefore challenged the church to use inclusive language guidelines to revise liturgies, prayers, hymns, and the Word of God itself. It was not acceptable to refer to God with male pronouns. Therefore, instead of "He," God became "S/ He." And then, in order to further Her/ His inclusiveness, God became "She~He~It." By changing the Biblical words and symbols about God, religious feminists *renamed* God. The god whom religious feminists began to worship was not the God revealed in the Bible and the God worshipped by orthodox Christians for centuries.[11]

Mary A. Kassian

We live in a culture that is drowning in gender confusion. The lines have become blurred and we are groping about trying to understand what it means for a man to be a man and a woman a woman, what it means for a man to be masculine and a woman feminine .... It is transparently clear that the cultural engineers that dominate the media, our educational system (from the preschools to the universities) and other strategic places of influence want to neutralize, if not eliminate, the gender distinctions and differences that God has hardwired into human beings (Gen 1:26–27). This is the consistent drumbeat heard again and again and unfortunately, the church has not been immune to the sound. Practicing homosexuals are now ordained as bishops. Divorced ministers continue in places of service as if nothing significant occurred when their marriage covenant was broken. Women (married, divorced, single, heterosexual and lesbian) now flock to seminaries and fill pulpits across the land declaring their liberation from the "oppressive" writings of the Bible. Even within evangelical fellowships women aspire to teaching positions that place them over men in Sunday Schools, Bible studies and local church worship

[11] *"The Challenge of Feminism"* Faith and Mission Volume 14 1996.

KEY QUOTES

services. The secular culture is shaping the Church more than sacred Scripture.[12]

Akin

Genesis 1:26–28 does teach that men and women equally bear the image of God but does not prove that one may hold ecclesiastical office simply because one bears the image of God. Acts 2:17–18 describes the outpouring of the Holy Spirit upon all God's people but does not prove that all who have the Spirit may hold ecclesiastical office. Galatians 3:28 declares that men and women are one in Christ, but that fact does not mean that women may hold ecclesiastical office any more than it means that the Christian husband is not the head of his wife (Eph. 5:23). 1 Timothy 2:11–12 clearly states that women are not to teach or have authority over men, and 1 Timothy 3:1–13 continues with an immediate application of this teaching to the offices of the church.[13]

Godfrey

The rejection of distinct gender roles ordained by the Creator is only one symptom of the world's defiance of the very notion of external, binding standards. Sinful man prefers to think of himself as an autonomous, rational individual, who is accountable to no one but himself and who has no other obligations than to maximize his own liberty, personal peace, and happiness... The present issue entails an entire culture's stance toward its Creator.[14]

Kostenberger

---

[12]Daniel Akin, *Journal Biblical Manhood and Womanhood* Volume 9 2004 p. 76.
[13]Robert Godfrey, *Journal for Biblical Manhood and Womanhood* Volume 1 1995
[14]*Paul's Pastoral Pronouncements Regarding Women's Roles in 1 Tim. 2:9–15 Faith and Mission*, Volume 14 1996 p. 37

KEY QUESTIONS

1. Does the Bible distinguish between the roles man and woman are meant to play? If so, what are the distinctions?

2. What should the attitude of a man be towards a woman and what should the attitude of a woman be to a man?

3. What scriptures would you use to show that men should never abuse or exploit women?

4. How does the submission of the Lord Jesus to the Father and His death on the cross illustrate the value of headship?

MAN'S PURPOSE

In the first lesson, we looked at the purpose of the creation of man and noted that the Bible teaches that man was created for God's glory. In this lesson we will look more carefully at that idea.

Created to Glorify God

David Hume, the famous Scottish philosopher, said, "It is an absurdity to believe that the Deity has human passions, and one of the lowest of human passions, a restless appetite for applause."[15] The Bible affirms the truth of at least one part of this quotation. Man does have a "restless appetite for applause" (2 Tim. 3:2). But what of Hume's claim that God seeks "applause"?

It should be noted that God "needs" nothing (Acts 17:24-25; Ps 50:10-12). He has no appetites which if unfulfilled will diminish or weaken Him. God did not make man because He needed praise. Nevertheless having created the cosmos and created man as part of that work of creation it is proper that man should praise Him. Just as it is proper that a child should be grateful to its parents so man should show his appreciation to his creator. A child that is ungrateful is a hateful thing. Theologians have debated for centuries why God created a universe that He knew would be

---

[15]*Dialogues Concerning Natural Religion.*

invaded by sin. Part of the answer must be that God considered it worthwhile if from His creatures there would be some that would choose to worship and serve Him. There is nothing unnatural in praising God nor is God diminished by His knowledge that He is worthy of His creature's praise. God does not need worship but He desires it.

Worship can be audible or inaudible. It can be oral or written. It may consist in acts of worship as well as words of worship. It can be solitary or corporate (1 Cor. 11:20). It can be expressed by the old (Heb. 11:21) and young (Matt. 21:16). By males or females. It may be offered in all sorts of places and situations. While its object is always God its subject can vary infinitely. The chief subject of worship is God the Father as creator (Acts 17:28; James 1:17; Rev. 4:11) and redeemer (Eph. 1:3; Col. 1:12–13; 1 Peter 1:3; Rev. 5:9–14). On the whole, we worship the Father through or in the name of the Son (Matt. 18:20; Rom. 5:2; Eph. 1:6; 1 Tim. 2:5; Heb. 4:14–5:10; 10:20). Exceptionally, the Son receives worship directly (1 Tim. 6:15-16). The references to men worshipping the Lord in the Gospels are primarily expressions of respect rather than ascribing worship to deity (e.g. Matt. 8:2; 9:18). But there were occasions when He was worshipped in a way that is reserved for deity (e.g. Matt. 28:9; Lk. 24:52; Jn 9:38). The Lord Jesus never prevented this worship so we may conclude that worship directly to Him as Son of God is legitimate. We never read in scripture of the Holy Spirit receiving worship. The Spirit energises worship (Rom. 2:28–29; 8:26–27; Eph. 2:18; Phil. 3:3; Jude 20).

The Hebrew word for "worship" (*shaha*) means "to bow down". The Greek word (*proskuneo*) means "to kiss the hand". Both words indicate that a sense of our inferiority to God ought to tinge our worship. Although there may be joy, praise ought to be characterised by reverence and holy fear. Thus while it is true that Christians of the Church age have an intimacy with God, worship is essentially the response of an inferior to a superior.

It is not really possible to glorify God if we act purely out of a sense of duty. While we ought to honour God; if we do so purely because we feel we have to and not because we want to, it will be worthless (Ps. 51:16-17).

Created to Serve God

The other reason for man's creation is that he may serve God. That service may take a huge variety of forms. It requires us to use whatever talents or abilities we have in a way that brings blessing to others – but the underlying aim is to serve God through our service of people. There is a strong hint in scripture however that our first duty is to our fellow Christians (Gal. 6:10; Jas 2:14-17) and thereafter to the world.

How we serve God is a personal matter. Because one serves God in one way does not mean that another may not serve God in a different way. We are prone to thinking that our form of service is the only one that matters. While social action such as alleviating poverty and hunger is a worthwhile exercise it should never eclipse the Christian's fundamental form of service which is to bring the gospel to the world. The Lord Jesus could have met the physical needs of everyone that He met but His declared mission was to "preach the gospel" (Lk 4:18). That said, true Christianity should be marked by compassion for the disadvantaged and we must never behave as the Priest and Levite behaved in the Parable of the Good Samaritan (Luke 10:30-37).

Although teaching and preaching are given great prominence among Christians, they are essentially forms of service. The expression "the ministry of the word" is only used once in scripture (Acts 6:4). The word "ministry" (*diakonia*) is used in the same context to describe the task of serving the widows (Acts 6:1). This emphasises that teaching the saints is no less or more exalted than looking after their physical needs.

Service for God can never be divorced from thankfulness to God. It is not anticipated that a Christian might worship but not serve or serve but not worship.

 ## KEY SCRIPTURES

For ye are bought with a price: therefore glorify God in your body, and in your spirit, which are God's.

1 Cor 6:20

22 And Samuel said, Hath the LORD *as great* delight in burnt offerings and sacrifices, as in obeying the voice of the LORD? Behold, to obey *is* better than sacrifice, *and* to hearken than the fat of rams. 23 For rebellion *is as* the sin of witchcraft, and stubbornness *is as* iniquity and idolatry.

1 Sam. 15:22–23

Master, which *is* the great commandment in the law? 37 Jesus said unto him, Thou shalt love the Lord thy God with all thy heart, and with all thy soul, and with all thy mind. 33 This is the first and great commandment. 39 And the second *is* like unto it, Thou shalt love thy neighbour as thyself. 40 On these two commandments hang all the law and the prophets.

Matt 22:36-40

23 But the hour cometh, and now is, when the true worshippers shall worship the Father in spirit and in truth: for the Father seeketh such to worship him. 24 God *is* a Spirit: and they that worship him must worship *him* in spirit and in truth.

John 4:23-24

15 By him therefore let us offer the sacrifice of praise to God continually, that is, the fruit of *our* lips giving thanks to his name. 16 But to do good and to communicate [to share what you have] forget not: for with such sacrifices God is well pleased.

Heb 13:15-16

KEY SCRIPTURES

And he said unto them, Go ye into all the world, and preach the gospel to every creature.

Mark 16:15

If I then, *your* Lord and Master, have washed your feet; ye also ought to wash one another's feet.

John 13:14

As we have therefore opportunity, let us do good unto all *men*, especially unto them who are of the household of faith.

Gal 6:10

KEY QUOTES

Biblical worship is often corrupted by boredom, lack of purpose, and non-participational behaviour which leads the congregation to go through the motions without genuine heart involvement. The opposite extreme offers little more than secular entertainment with a religious veneer, a packaged plastic program so perfect and professional that even the most sincere worshipper can scarcely break through its shrink-wrapped design to get his hands on true worship. [16]

Kenneth Gangel

Christian people have been on the front lines of social change ever since the beginning, when Roman Christians risked their lives to rescue infants who had been left to die by their parents in the hills surrounding the city... In the nineteenth century, liberal Christianity said that salvation came through social action, creating the "social" gospel. Seeking to

---

[16] Kenneth Gangel, *"Re-examining Biblical Worship"* Bibliotheca Sacra Volume 142 p162.

KEY QUOTES

preserve the great truths of orthodox Christianity, most conservative Christians came to feel that any expression of a social gospel was liberal and defamed Scripture. We must not fall into that trap. Salvation comes through faith, not through actions and works, but true faith always manifests itself in action, including legitimate social action.[17]

R C Sproul

---

[17] *Before the Face of God Book 3: A Daily Guide for Living from the Old Testament.*

??? KEY QUESTIONS

1. Some say man evolved. If so, is there any reason for or purpose to human existence?

2. If God could foresee that man would fail, why did He nevertheless create man?

3. What is worship?

4. What forms of service can we give to God?

MAN'S
PINNACLE

The Lord Jesus was the Son of God before He took up humanity (Jn 1:1). His humanity however began at conception and was manifested at birth. He was not conceived by the union of man with woman. He was conceived of the Holy Spirit (Matt 1:20). This was in fulfilment of the prophecy in Genesis 3:14-15 which speaks of the Lord Jesus prophetically as the seed of the woman. Normally children are said to be the seed of their father (e.g. Gen 9:9; Lk 1:55) but the Lord Jesus had no earthly father. He was however Mary's son (Mk 6:3) since she conceived and bore the Lord Jesus. He was moreover of the tribe of Judah through Mary's lineage and therefore heir to David's throne and promises (Rom. 1:3). While it seemed outwardly that the Lord was the son of Joseph and while Joseph took responsibility for Him (e.g. Jn 1:45), Luke makes it clear that His humanity owed nothing to Joseph (Lk 3:23).

The Bible teaches that He had true humanity. He had flesh which could be pierced by nails (Ps 22:16). He had hair which could be plucked out (Is 50:6). If wounded, He bled (Jn 19:34); if deprived of food, He hungered (Matt 21:18;Lk 4:2); if sorrowful, He wept (Jn 11:35) and if tired, He slept (Matt 8:24).

Yet He was divine as well as human (Col. 2:9). As such He could do things that ordinary humans cannot do. For example, He could walk on water (Matt 14:25), change it into wine (Jn 2:9) and calm it when stormy (Mk 4:39). He knew what people were thinking (Lk 6:8) not only as they thought it but before they thought it (Jn 6:64). He never relinquished His divinity when He took up humanity.

Our humanity is sinful humanity. The Lord Jesus' humanity was holy humanity (Heb 7:26). He did not sin (Heb. 4:15) and could not sin (1 Jn 3:5). We sin and are unable not to sin. He was unable to sin. Sin has caused all sorts of genetic and physical imperfections which are transmitted from generation to generation. The Lord however was not a descendant of Adam. He was the "second Man" (1 Cor 15:45, 47) and His humanity was not subject to Adam's legacy of weakness and disease. He had perfect humanity.

Alexander Pope the poet said "to err is human". Those errors are not necessarily sinful errors. We make innocent mistakes. The Lord Jesus however because He was truly divine as well as truly human was not prone to errors or misjudgments. He was truly perfect. This should provoke us to worship.

We cannot fully explain how divinity and humanity co-existed and there are many difficulties in understanding the "mystery of godliness" (1 Tim 3:16). But His humanity was a necessary precondition of His self-sacrifice on Calvary and without His humanity we would still be in our sins (Heb 2:9).

 ## KEY SCRIPTURES

20 But while he thought on these things, behold, the angel of the Lord appeared unto him in a dream, saying, Joseph, thou son of David, fear not to take unto thee Mary thy wife: for that which is conceived in her is of the Holy Ghost. 21 And she shall bring forth a son, and thou shalt call his name JESUS: for he shall save his people from their sins.

Matt 1:20–21

35 And the angel answered and said unto her, The Holy Ghost shall come upon thee, and the power of the Highest shall overshadow thee: therefore also that holy thing which shall be born of thee shall be called the Son of God.

Luke 1:35

7 But made himself of no reputation, and took upon him the form of a servant, and was made in the likeness of men: 8 And being found in fashion as a man, he humbled himself, and became obedient unto death, even the death of the cross. 9 Wherefore God also hath highly exalted him, and given him a name which is above every name: 10 That at the name of Jesus every knee should bow, of *things* in heaven, and *things* in earth, and *things* under the earth; 11 And *that* every tongue should confess that Jesus Christ *is* Lord, to the glory of God the Father.

Phil 2:7–11

9 For in him dwelleth all the fulness of the Godhead bodily. 10 And ye are complete in him, which is the head of all principality and power:

Col 2:9–10

But we see Jesus, who was made a little lower than the angels for the suffering of death, crowned with glory and honour; that he by the grace of God should taste death for every man.

Hebrews 2:9

KEY SCRIPTURES

And without controversy great is the mystery of godliness: God was manifest in the flesh, justified in the Spirit, seen of angels, preached unto the Gentiles, believed on in the world, received up into glory.

1 Timothy 3:16

KEY QUOTES

The miracle was not in His birth but in His conception. While the Holy Spirit was the power that enabled Mary to conceive yet He is never said to be the Father of Christ, nor must we ever believe that Christ was part God and part Man. No! He was wholly Man and wholly God. The incarnation was not the impartation of the divine essence to Mary for the Divine essence is intransmissible. Rather it was that the Son of God partook of blood and flesh thus uniting two natures in one person, yet these two are never confused but always remain distinct. Although Mary was a fallen creature like all others of the human race and as such was never said to be sinless, yet the power of the Spirit that enabled her to conceive also preserved the One conceived from all contamination so that He was as holy when born as when conceived.

Albert McShane[18]

He was born in an obscure village, the child of a peasant woman. He worked in a carpenter shop until He was thirty. Then for three years He was an itinerant preacher. He never wrote a book. He never held an office. He never had a family or owned a house. He never went to college. He never travelled two hundred miles from the place where He was born. He never did one of the things that usually accompany greatness. He had no credentials but Himself. He was only thirty-three when the tide of

[18]*The Person of Christ* (Gospel Tract Publications) pp. 54-55.

KEY QUOTES

public opinion turned against Him. His friends ran away. He was nailed to a cross between two thieves. When He was dead, He was laid in a borrowed grave through the pity of a friend. Nineteen centuries have come and gone, and today He is the central figure of the human race, and the leader of the column of progress. I am far within the mark when I say that all the armies that ever marched, all the navies that ever sailed, all the parliaments that ever sat, all the kings that ever reigned, put together, have not affected the life of man on earth as has that One Solitary Life.

Phillips Brooks

When the Word 'became flesh' His deity was not abandoned, or reduced, or contracted, nor did He cease to exercise the divine functions which had been His before. It is He, we are told, who sustains the creation in ordered existence, and who gives and upholds all life (Col. 1:17; Heb. 1:3; Jn. 1:4), and these functions were certainly not in abeyance during his time on earth. When He came into the world he 'emptied himself' of outward glory (Phil. 2:7; Jn. 17:5), and in that sense He 'became poor' (2 Cor. 8:9), but this does not at all imply a curtailing of His divine powers, such as the so-called kenosis theories would suggest. The New Testament stresses rather that the Son's deity was not reduced through the incarnation. In the man Christ Jesus, says Paul, 'dwelleth *all the fullness of the Godhead bodily*' (Col. 2:9; *cf.* 1:19).

The incarnation of the Son of God, then, was not a diminishing of deity, but an acquiring of manhood. It was not that God the Son came to indwell a human being, as the Spirit was later to do. (To assimilate incarnation to indwelling is the essence of the Nestorian heresy.) It was rather that the Son in person began to live a fully human life. He did not simply clothe himself in a human body, taking the place of its soul, as Apollinaris maintained; He took to himself a human soul as well as a human body, *i.e.* He entered into the experience of human psychical life as well as of human physical life. His manhood was complete; He became 'the *man* Christ Jesus' (1 Tim. 2:5; *cf.* Gal. 4:4; Heb. 2:14, 17). And his manhood is

KEY QUOTES

permanent. Though now exalted, He 'continueth to be, God and man in two distinct natures, and one person, for ever' (*Westminster Shorter Catechism*, Q. 21; *cf.* Heb. 7:24).[2]

New Bible Dictionary

---

[19]*New Bible Dictionary (3rd ed.)* p503–504.

?? KEY QUESTIONS

1. Did the Son of God exist before Jesus was born?

2. How do we know that the Lord Jesus was truly human?

3. If the Lord Jesus could sin, what would the implications be?

4. Could the Lord Jesus have made an innocent mistake? If not, why not?